Original title:
The Necklace's Heart

Copyright © 2025 Creative Arts Management OÜ
All rights reserved.

Author: Benjamin Caldwell
ISBN HARDBACK: 978-1-80586-224-6
ISBN PAPERBACK: 978-1-80586-696-1

Mysteries in Light

In shadows deep, a sparkle lies,
An ordinary tale, disguised with sighs.
A gem so grand, yet lost in fate,
Its value found far too late.

A lady pranced in silk and lace,
With dreams that danced in a brightened space.
But oh, that shimmer turned to air,
As laughter took its foolish share.

She borrowed more than just the bling,
But hopes that cheered with each small fling.
A mix-up here, a hiccup there,
With glee and gasps filling the air.

When truth unravels with a twist,
What silly messes can't be missed?
In tales of treasure come and go,
Life's riches often steal the show.

Glistening Facades

A shimmer here, a sparkle there,
Diamonds dance without a care.
But beneath the glow and gleam,
Lies a tale that makes you scream!

A planning queen with budget tight,
She struts around like fairy light.
But in the end, oh what a farce,
It's plastic hearts in sparkly jars!

A Tapestry of Glittering Secrets

Behind the veil of glittered lies,
She dons the glitz with sly disguise.
While sipping tea in fancy halls,
Her secret's bound to cause some brawls!

Friends think her fortune blooms so vast,
While she's clipping coupons fast.
The laughter echoes, fills the air,
Her glimmer dims, but who would care?

Shadows Behind the Shine

In pageantry of beaded gloss,
Lurks a suit with zero floss.
She shines as bright as summer sun,
But the truth's a comical run!

Her jewels gleam, oh what a show!
But pawning them, she steals the glow.
With glitter trails and awkward slips,
Her stories lead to laughing quips!

The Lure of Opulent Desires

Allure of charms, a flashy spree,
She dives headfirst, oh woe is she!
In search of treasure, bling, and gold,
But finds the tales too rich to hold!

Her lavish dreams, a crazy quest,
Yet thrift shops greet her as the best.
With charm and wit, she dodges cracks,
Her laughter echoes, no looking back!

Adorned but Undone

In fancy dress, she spins around,
A sparkly gem, she's tightly wound.
But every twist, a clothesline crack,
Her bauble's bling is under attack.

With every dance, a laugh erupts,
A battle with sequins, what's not corrupt?
Her pearls flee far, from neck to knee,
And diamonds scatter like they're free!

A Legacy Bound in a Mirror

Behold the glass, a grand façade,
Where glimmers lie and masks applaud.
She posed for glam, her best small feat,
But missed the chair and met her seat.

Reflections warped, her style excessive,
The mirror laughed, so very possessive.
"Who's this?" it chimed with a sneering grin,
"Another fool lost in fashion's spin?"

Glimmers of Glamour and Grief

On party nights, the jewels parade,
With winks and laughter, a grand charade.
Yet under lights, the truth would spark,
That one lost gem lay in the dark.

"Oh dear," she mused, a tear of glee,
"Was that my earring, or just debris?"
Her friends all snickered, the mood was light,
As she tripped again, what a sight!

The Illusion of Perfect Radiance

She donned the crown, her regal grace,
But found her shoe tagged as 'not the place'.
With every step, her poise a bloom,
A curse of glam that spelt her doom.

The tiara slipped, the sparkle waned,
In brightest light, her pride was drained.
"Just call it art!" she laughed with flare,
"A masterstroke in fumbled air!"

Ambivalence in Adornment

In a box of sparkles, she saved her days,
Each gem a secret, in funny displays.
Rings that promise dreams, yet make her sigh,
Why wear the weight? She'd rather fly.

Each bracelet jingles, like laughter's own tune,
Yet feels like a monkey on her afternoon.
Should she flaunt her jewels, or send them away?
A bangle's dilemma turns bright into gray.

Echoing Traces

A shimmer of memories, in layers of gold,
Every piece whispers tales, half-brazen, half-bold.
She dons a locket, full of half-spoken words,
While her dog thinks it's lunch, staring at birds.

With pearls on her neck, folks notice and gawk,
She trips on her own glam, like a comic block.
For every wrong turn, she wears a bright grin,
Laughing at jewels, and the mess she's in.

Glimmering Surfaces

Her charm bracelet jangles, like a door full of keys,
Unlocking the flops and the fun little wheeze.
Every charm has a story, like a quirky friend,
Some memories cozy, while others just bend.

The diamond so bright, yet it's not all it seems,
It sparkles and shines, but hides all her dreams.
In moments of laughter, she questions the bling,
Is it worth the weight? Or just another fling?

Shadowed Liaisons

A ring that's too tight, it pulls at her woes,
It's snug and it's funny, as everyone knows.
"Wear this!" they chant, as she sinks with a grin,
A weight on her finger, but freedom within.

With brooches that giggle and earrings that chuckle,
She wanders through days, like a flustered luckle.
In the dance of her jewels, all worries are catchy,
For laughter's a treasure, and life's just a patchy.

Jewels of Regret

Shiny baubles in a drawer,
Forgotten treasures, nothing more.
Promises of glamour, all in vain,
Now just dust, a hint of pain.

Once they sparkled, oh so bright,
Now they giggle, out of sight.
Each piece whispers, 'Where's the fun?'
In the sorrow, I now run.

Charm of the Untold

A tale of sparkle, lost and found,
A ribbon of laughter all around.
Behind each gem, a story lies,
Of clumsy falls and silly cries.

Mysteries wrapped in fancy bows,
Awkward moments that nobody knows.
Yet here I stand, a jester's hat,
Dancing lightly with my cat.

Reflections of Longing

In the mirror, I see my dreams,
Reflecting wishes, or so it seems.
Each twinkling light, a silver lie,
Chasing shadows that rush by.

Hoping for grace, but wearing clumsiness,
Winking at fate with cheeky finesse.
Oh, the giggles of wanting more,
In a patchwork life, who keeps the score?

Vows Entwined

We made some promises, sweet and bright,
To wear the jewels, oh what a sight!
But life's a circus, and I can't cope,
Fumbling my dreams with a dash of hope.

In tangled ribbons, we twirl and spin,
Laughing at how we can't quite win.
The vows we share, a comical fate,
With each mishap, we celebrate.

Jewels of Melancholy

In a box of trinkets, piled high,
Lies a charm that makes the eyebrows fly.
Once sparkled bright, now gathers dust,
A treasure trove of misplaced trust.

A pearl that thought it was a star,
Now just a bauble in a jar.
The gold once glimmered, now it snores,
Tired of waiting for its tours!

Forgotten Luminescence

There's a locket holding memories dear,
But now it shrinks away in fear.
Once it danced in the evening sun,
Now it just hopes it will be fun.

A diamond's laugh, a sapphire's frown,
They sit in silence, wearing down.
When did they last take a spin?
Oh, where's the laughter that should begin?

Lament of Luxuries

A bracelet jingles, but not with glee,
It whines and mutters, 'Look at me!'
"Once I dazzled, oh what a show,
Now I'm stuck here, feeling low."

Earrings whisper tales of grace,
But get embarrassed, hide their face.
In the dark, they plot and plan,
To one day shine, like they began.

Fragments of Yesterday

A brooch recalls the dances held,
But now it fumbles, mildly felled.
Once it wore the crown with pride,
Now it dreams of a joyful ride.

The past is sparkly, fun, and bright,
Now it yearns for a chance to light.
Each piece a tale, a joke untold,
Waiting for laughter to break the mold.

Shimmering Secrets

A glimmer caught her wandering eye,
In a box of lace and dreams awry.
She wore it once, then tossed aside,
While the mirror winked, her guilty pride.

In parties grand, she'd strut and glow,
Though her purse was light, she stole the show.
With borrowed strands from friends in glee,
That twinkling charm, a sight to see.

But secrets hid in folds of gold,
Too many tales she spun and told.
The laughter echoed, her fate a jest,
Draped in humor, she felt most blessed.

In the end, the sparkle fades away,
Yet memories dance and brightly stay.
For joy in jest, she knew the cost,
In shiny charms, she laughed and lost.

Chains of Destiny

A laugh rang out when she stepped in line,
Wearing links of fate that shimmered fine.
Each jingle told a tale of its own,
And a chorus of giggles her jewels had grown.

The shopkeeper chuckled, "That's quite the flair!"
As she balanced her burdens with utmost care.
To snag a compliment, she danced around,
But tripped on her fortune, fell to the ground.

With chains of laughter wrapped close to her heart,
Every blunder became a true art.
Life's little pratfalls became grand designs,
In a world where humor forever shines.

She wore her bling with a wink and a grin,
In her wild adventure, she found her win.
For every stumble, a giggle would rise,
The chains of destiny, full of surprise.

Illusions in Silver

The silver sparkled, like stars on a whim,
A ruse so clever, it made her head swim.
"Oh darling," she laughed, with a twirl so spry,
These illusions delight, but oh, how they lie!

Upon her wrist, the shimmering grace,
A circus of wonders dressed in lace.
With each turn and twist, they'd gleam and sparkle,
Yet reality whispered, "Oh, what a farc'l!"

In mirrors reflecting her charm and sass,
She wondered aloud, "Will this moment last?"
But laughter brought light to her glimmery tale,
In the game of pretense, she'd never fail.

The truth of the glow? A penny stored tight,
Her spirit was rich, shining ever so bright.
In illusions of silver, she danced like a queen,
Oh the joy in her folly, simply unseen!

Threads of Fortune

In threads of fortune, she weaved her delight,
A tapestry bright, what a curious sight!
Each stitch told a story, a giggle, a cheer,
In the looms of life, there's nothing to fear.

She'd strut on the street, golden threads in her hair,
While the folks around couldn't help but stare.
"Who dressed this clown?" they whispered with glee,
But she laughed out loud, "Oh, can't you see?"

With fortune's fabric wrapped snug in her heart,
She spun tales of wonder, right from the start.
Every misstep turned into a dance,
With humor her armor, she'd take every chance.

Through stitches of joy, her spirit would weave,
In the grand show of life, never to grieve.
For threads of fortune, both wobbly and bright,
Made her twinkle, drifting into the night.

Ephemeral Embellishments

A sparkly trinket, oh what a find,
It glitters and glimmers, it's one of a kind.
But wait, it's plastic, just a cheap toy,
Yet on my wrist, it gives me such joy.

In the light, it dazzles, a shimmering sight,
A fashion faux pas, but it feels so right.
Friends all gather, and oh, what a laugh,
As my sparkly treasure takes a fine photograph.

Mirror, oh mirror, don't tell me the truth,
This shiny bauble holds no real proof.
Like candy it melts, this charm won't last,
But oh, in this moment, I'm having a blast!

The laughter escapes, as I strut and I play,
Dressing up fancy in my glittery array.
A jewel that is fleeting, but laughter stays near,
In this fleeting bling, I find lasting cheer.

Radiant Whispers

A necklace of whispers that's shiny and bright,
It jangles and clatters, such a curious sight.
But under the lights, oh what a disaster,
It's just old popcorn, my fashion's master.

Sparkling like diamonds, or so I pretend,
With every swing, my fashion could end.
"Darling, how lovely!" my friends all agree,
But I know the truth, it was free from a spree.

Charming and stylish, yet slightly askew,
My trinket collection would make you go 'ew!'
Yet here I am shining, in glittery glee,
Crafted by dreams and a wild fantasy.

So let's raise a glass to the silly and fun,
To necklaces made of popcorn, we've won!
With radiance bordering on sheer fantasy,
I wear my creations, oh can't you see?

Chained Promises

With chains made of promise, my heart starts to race,
A treasure so shiny, yet lacking in grace.
"Oh look at my pendant!" I say with a grin,
While secretly wishing I'd just saved my win.

A bargain that dazzles, or so I had thought,
But really it's clutter from all I had bought.
In this crazy chaos, a giggle we share,
As we prance with our baubles, with nary a care.

Yet soon comes the moment, the charm starts to break,
A quick tug, and oh no! It's a terrible quake.
The laughter erupts, as the pieces all fall,
A lesson in jewelry, I learned from it all.

So here's to the trinkets, the fun and the strife,
In friendship and laughter, we find the real life.
For chains made of laughter, they hold us so dear,
With silly old charms, let's spread joy and cheer!

Essence of Allure

A glimmering bauble, oh what a delight,
It beckons the eye in the soft, evening light.
Yet its essence is fleeting, like bubbles in air,
It's merely a trinket, but oh, do I care?

In laughter we dance, with jewelry askew,
Each piece is a story, each laugh is brand new.
A charm that's not golden, with history strange,
But together we sparkle, such a jubilant range.

Fashion's a circus, and we're all the clowns,
With necklaces twirling like tax refund gowns.
So let's raise our cups, to the shimmer, the jest,
For the essence of allure lies in friendship's zest.

In glitzy confusion, our hearts find the way,
To cherish the moments and laugh every day.
For nothing's more precious than joy that can spark,
In this wild adventure, we wander, we hark!

Pendant of Longing

A pendant dangles, swinging low,
Dreaming of places it can't go.
It shimmies in the morning light,
Wishing it could take a flight.

It whispers tales of nights so grand,
Of parties where it took a stand.
But alas, it's stuck on my neck,
Feeling all the social wreck!

It rolls its eyes at dusty shelves,
And sighs at all the dusty elves.
"Let's dance!" it pleads with all its might,
But my feet just won't ignite.

So here we sit, both quite forlorn,
Living life just like a thorn.
Yet still it beams, a gleeful jest,
For it can surely say, "I'm dressed!"

Enigma in Gold

An enigma wrapped in shiny gold,
A mystery, or so I'm told.
It clinks along with a playful sound,
As if it knows it's glory-bound.

It giggles at all the silly fakes,
And shakes its charm for friendship's sakes.
In every sparkle, a riddle hides,
Too goofy for pretentious rides.

At times it dreams of fashion trends,
Wishing for fame, but who pretends?
In closets dark, it sometimes stumbles,
Over forgotten and dusty fumbles.

Yet still it shines with a cheeky grin,
"I'll be the star, just let me in!"
So here we are, so snug and bold,
Me and my enigma wrapped in gold.

Tapestry of Wishes

A tapestry woven with giggles and dreams,
Threads of laughter unravel in gleams.
Each knot tells a tale of silly delight,
Stitched together all through the night.

The colors dance like a playful crew,
Tickled by stardust and morning dew.
"Oh, to be worn!" the fabric pleads,
Yet waits on the shelf while my heart speeds.

It can't understand my fashion plight,
Why I prefer jeans to its soft invite.
So it laughs at me — "A choice so bland!
Let's strut together and make a stand!"

But still the fabric gathers dust,
Wishing and hoping, it's a must.
And haunts my closet with a funny frown,
"Where's the fun in this old gown?"

Silken Threads of Time

Silken threads that pull and tease,
Tickle my mind like a gentle breeze.
They weave and twist in odd designs,
Making each moment a grand surprise.

As time unravels in graceful spins,
The fabric laughs and giggles within.
"I could dress you up," it slyly hints,
"You've just got to look past the tints!"

But I hesitate, for style's a maze,
Caught in the riddle of fashion's craze.
"What if I trip? What if I fall?"
The silk just chuckles, "Just give it your all!"

So here's to the threads that dance in style,
Making me wear a funny smile.
For in the tangle, we find our rhyme,
Living hilariously, one thread at a time.

Beauty's Paradox

In the mirror I see so fair,
A crown of chaos upon my hair.
My charm is bright, but oh, the cost,
I bought a dress, but socks are lost.

With makeup skills, I tried to slay,
But ended up in disarray.
A lovely laugh at my own plight,
I'm a fashionista, just not tonight!

They say perfection's just a game,
But messy hair is half the fame.
A little sparkle, some flare to flaunt,
Yet here I am, a style savant!

So hats off to the glamorous gaze,
For beauty loves to set ablaze.
Though chaos reigns, I'll wear a smile,
A funny tale, my life's true style.

Mirage of Magnificence

With grandeur dreams upon my mind,
A glitzy life I hope to find.
A diamond dress, oh what a thrill,
Too bad it's plastic, not a real frill!

I twirl around in sugary gowns,
Untangling jewels as my face frowns.
I step on heels, they break in two,
A statue's pose, while stuck like glue!

In a whirlwind of sequins and flair,
I trip on pride, and oh, beware!
The laughter echoes through the halls,
As elegance tumbles, and chaos calls.

Still, I plod with grace and charm,
Pretending these missteps won't harm.
A mirror's jest, a comical dance,
This marbled life, my funny chance!

Heirlooms of the Heart

Oh, grandma's pearls that itch and tug,
I wear them proud, though they feel snug.
With vintage outfits stitched with care,
My style's a puzzle—oh, beware!

I strut around, a posh charade,
In gowns inherited, now slightly frayed.
Each thread's a tale, a giggle or two,
But fashion's timeless—like a zoo!

With tulle and lace, I swan so bright,
Though slip on steps may steal the night.
I laugh aloud at every snare,
For heirlooms make me brave to dare.

So here I stand, a fusion rare,
With wit and whimsy dancing in air.
My family's quirks are treasures, too,
As heirlooms laugh and style anew.

Elegance Unraveled

As I dress in silk, oh so divine,
Threads unravel, crossing the line.
I pose with poise, a royal decree,
Till snagging beads shout, "Look at me!"

The posture grand, but the hem is short,
I trip on glamour, what a sport!
In the chaos, I spin and twirl,
Elegance slips—oh, what a whirl!

A cocktail dress charms with its sheen,
But oops! It's smudged with spilled cuisine.
With baffled friends, we burst through mirth,
Laughter echoes, a party's worth!

The night unfolds with blunders bright,
In fashion's jest, I find delight.
So here's to the slips, the fun and the cheer,
For elegance is tangled but oh-so-dear.

Emotions Entwined in Sterling

She donned a sparkler, oh so bright,
Every glance felt just right,
But tripped on flair, she caught her shoe,
And danced the tango, no one knew.

Gems on her neck, but hair went wild,
A strut so grand, like a giddy child,
She twirled and spun, a dizzy spree,
Polished silver and giggles, oh me!

At parties, oh, the tales she spun,
With every twist, a pun came undone,
Laughter bubbled, like soda pop,
She wore her laughter, a jewel non-stop.

In the end, it was clear to see,
That her trinkets and laughs were all for free,
Charm and folly twinkled bright,
Her gem-filled heart, a sheer delight!

The Hidden Cost of Adornments

With pearls and glitters, she felt so grand,
But oh, the weight of that heavy band!
She wore them all with flair and grace,
Yet tripped on air in the awkward space.

Each bauble sparkled, her confidence grew,
But in her sandwich, a stone she chewed!
Her jaw went slack, her eyes went wide,
As lunch became a diamond ride.

Fancy affairs brought her quite the fuss,
But who knew rhinestones could create such a buzz?
She posed for photos, a gem-studded queen,
Yet lost her purse in a fashion routine.

Her friends all giggled, "What a sight to see!"
As she juggled jewels and missed the tea,
A lesson learned in a sparkle burst,
That laughter's worth more than any jewel or thirst!

Silhouettes of Splendor

In silks and jewels, she danced with flair,
But realized too late, she forgot to wear,
Her shoes were swapped for slippers quite meek,
As she cha-cha'd away, a dazzling sneak.

Glitzy and glam, the crowd went wild,
Her moves were fierce, yet so utterly mild,
A spin, a drop, then oops! She tripped,
And in that moment, her chicness flipped.

With crown atop, she felt so bold,
But then her wig slipped, truth be told,
A laughter wave washed over the hall,
As she embraced her faux pas with a hilarious fall.

A silhouette of splendid jest,
Bringing smiles on every quest,
For jewels may shine, but grace the best,
Is laughter shared, the ultimate fest!

Worn Yet Untamed

With bracelets rattling, she dashed to the door,
A whirlwind of charms, but who could ask for more?
The bells on her ankles jingled with cheer,
As she lost her patience (and shoe!) with a sneer.

Each gem she flaunted was a story to tell,
About the days when she stumbled and fell,
Laughter echoed, her pride took a hit,
But in the end, she just rolled with it.

She wore a tiara but felt like a clown,
As her friend yelled, "Is that sparkle a frown?"
Together they giggled, holding on tight,
To a world of madness, dressed up just right.

So here's to the worn, the wild, and free,
Embracing the chaos with glee and esprit,
For when jewels are not just for show,
It's the heart that sparkles, you know!

Precious Echoes of Distant Days

In a box of sparkles, oh so fine,
A treasure was lost, or was it a sign?
Gold glittered bright, but oh what a weight,
Silly mistakes? Can make one feel great!

Worn at the gala, a dazzling charm,
Floated like a dream, causing some harm.
A twist of the wrist, then off it did fly,
A tumble in chaos, oh my, oh my!

We chased after sparkles, with laughter and cheer,
Dodging the crowds, feeling quite clear.
But alas! A fierce cat with a pounce and a leap,
Claimed glory and shimmer, then fell fast asleep!

So here's to the days filled with shiny delight,
When what glimmers bright can dance in the night.
In memories stored, just laughter remains,
What's precious is silly, and that's how it gains!

A Symphony of Broken Brilliance

A glittery joke, oh what a sight!
Lost in my dreams, I twinkled with fright.
Dancing around with a clip of my hair,
Suddenly missing, oh, was it a flare?

A caterwaul symphony, fell from my ear,
A clumsy crescendo, igniting great cheer.
With every willowy twirl, a drop and a crash,
I laughed 'til I cried in a hysterical flash!

The villagers gawked at the chaos I wrought,
As gems rolled like marbles, oh what a plot!
In folly I pranced, fully unaware,
When glittering treasures danced through the air!

But just like my charm, life sparkles and glows,
With chaos in tow, how joyously it flows!
So raise up a toast to the brilliance we break,
For each little blunder, a memory we make!

In the Heart of Glistening Desire

Once found in a dream, a charm of misfortune,
Winking and blinking from its little cocoon.
Sought after fiercely, oh how it did spin,
Holding my heart, but it won't let me in!

Adventures were promised, oh sparkling delight,
To wear it with pride, oh, just felt so right!
But then came the rain, and a hop from the guy,
A tumble, a splash, and away it did fly!

I chased after raindrops, with giggles and speed,
As puddles embraced me, no worries nor creed.
With a squish and a splash, the charm met its fate,
Oh, laughter emerging, wasn't it great?

So here's to the trials of all that we chase,
From desires so bright, to the smiles on our face!
Let's toast to the journey, its glitter and glare,
For every lost treasure reveals how we care!

The Lament of Luminescent Regrets

In shadowy corners, a pearl took a fall,
Wrapped in mischief, it towered so tall.
Thoughts of grand plans and shining delights,
Until one fateful night, those plans took to flight!

The whispers of gossip, oh what a sound,
As each glimmering regret tumbled around.
When laughter turned serious, I felt such a crunch,
As I bobbed in the moonlight, a shimmering punch!

Worries like feathers, they drift in the breeze,
But my weighty regrets just wouldn't appease.
Each missing bauble, they chuckled aloud,
"Who needs shiny gems when a joke's in the crowd?"

So here's to the laughter, the jesting, the fun,
For life is just sparkles 'til the last race is run.
Let's embrace our glimmers, with all of their weight,
For each shiny tear is just fate's little bait!

Adornments of Desire

In a drawer, sparkles hide,
A shiny treasure, oh what pride!
Worn once for a dance so grand,
Now it's lost, can't understand.

It dangles here, it shines so bright,
Thought a queen, danced all night.
Now it gathers dust and sighs,
A gem of dreams, oh how it lies!

Echoes of Elegance

A locket swings with tales to tell,
Of weekend parties—oh so swell!
It once danced at every fête,
Now on the shelf, it's just first-rate.

A bracelet sparkles like a star,
Worn once to fame, but now? Too far!
It fancies itself a grand affair,
But nobody's noticed it there!

Trinket of Dreams

Once it twinkled with every glance,
Now it collects dust with no chance.
An eager charm from days of yore,
  Now just a napkin on the floor.

It was a ring, a shiny blast,
Glimmering memories of the past.
And though it's lost its former flair,
  It still sits proud in stale air!

Radiance Enshrined

A pearl necklace, so divine,
Worn once to show my dazzling shine.
Now it's tangled, a hopeless case,
"Oh dear", I sigh, "What a disgrace!"

Its shimmer claims a timeless jest,
Too fancy for my humble quest.
It laughs at me, I laugh along,
For in my heart, it still feels strong!

Shattered Illusions

In a box of shiny things,
She thought she'd found her dreams.
But every gem and precious ring,
Were just for sparkly schemes.

With a laugh, she tossed them high,
A glittered mess in the air.
"I'll find my fortune by and by,"
While dodging gems everywhere!

When asked of riches, she just grinned,
Her heart was light, her purse was thin.
"Trust me dear, it's not the end,"
"Just watch me spin and spin!"

So she danced beneath the stars,
With laughter loud and mirth divine.
Who needs bling or fancy cars?
Life's a joke, and I'm just fine!

Glisten and Gloom

A jewel that sparkled bright and bold,
Held tales of glamour, or so she thought.
But under the shine, secrets unfold,
A tale of troubles that never sought.

In a party dress, she wore that bling,
Pretending life was grand and fair.
But every wink and every fling,
Led to mishaps and quirky air!

"Is it real?" a friend asked with glee,
She winked and whispered, "Ah, my dear!
It's fool's gold, but can't you see?
It glistens more when there's no fear!"

So they laughed and danced through the night,
With funny stories from days of yore.
Gloom faded fast with pure delight,
Together they'd always want more!

Threads of Yesteryear

Once she wore that fancy thread,
Tales of elegance it spun.
But all the laughter soon was bred,
From tales of things that came undone.

"Oh these pearls, they're quite a hoax!"
She'd giggle as she rolled her eyes.
"Last dinner, I fed all the folks,
With a soup of sequins and lies!"

Stitches frayed as friendships grew,
In the quilt of joyous days.
With every laugh, she bent the truth,
Weaving fun in funny ways!

So here's to threads, that won't unbind,
In laughter, we stitch anew.
In every twinkle, joy we find,
Life's a tapestry, just like you!

Tokens of Forgotten Dreams

In her attic, treasures piled,
Old tokens from forgotten days.
With a chuckle, she felt beguiled,
At memories lost in a haze.

"Here's a button, won't it shine?
And a brooch that looks like cheese!"
She showed her friends with glee divine,
"Who knew dreams could come with fleas?"

But as they laughed, the truth unfurled,
What mattered most was shared delight.
In every silly, crazy whirl,
Their hearts glowed bold in the night!

So raise a glass to oddball finds,
To dreams that make us laugh and scream.
In these tokens, love unwinds,
A funny yet heartfelt beam!

Precious Deceptions

In glitter's grip, a tale we weave,
Where baubles dance, and hearts believe.
A charming smile, a trusting glance,
With clever tricks, we all advance.

A diamond's shine, a ruse we name,
Behind the scenes, who plays this game?
A fake facade, a silly jest,
Who knew a spark would bring such jest?

The laughter rolls like jewels unchained,
Over missteps that left us stained.
Yet in the chaos, joy ignites,
Our foolish hearts take to new heights.

With every twist, a grin appears,
We toast to fortune, then to cheers!
For in our folly, we find the art,
In precious things, we play our part.

Whisper of Glamour

Oh, glittering dreams on a paper crown,
With sparkly chats in the bustling town.
A slip on the floor sends gasps around,
And laughter erupts without a sound.

In sequined skirts, we spin and twirl,
While fabric flares, confusion swirls.
A dash for show, a dash for flair,
But who's that laughing? Oh, I declare!

With every glance, a story grows,
As charm and chaos dance in rows.
We sip on dreams, such fancy wine,
In whispers soft, we claim what's mine.

Yet when the dusk brings tired grins,
We'll trade our woes for silly sins.
In whispered night, we find our spark,
In glamour's grip, we hit the mark.

Fractured Splendor

Once a jewel, a treasure grand,
Now just bits lost in the sand.
With each mishap, we laugh it off,
As jokes collide, and chuckles scoff.

Oh, the wonder of shimmering lies,
As we adorn our foolish ties.
A tangled strand, a charming mess,
Who would have thought? We love this stress!

Through broken dreams and giggles bright,
We find the fun in every plight.
With humor's balm, we mend our pride,
In splendor flawed, we'll take the ride.

So raise a glass to fractured grace,
In every stumble, find your place.
Embrace the freaks, the quirks, the art,
For joy resides in every heart.

Twinkling Sorrows

When laughter shines, and tears release,
A glimpse of joy brings us such peace.
With glistening dreams, we find our way,
In shadows light, we laugh and sway.

The giggles hide our little pains,
While shiny thoughts break off our chains.
In the sparkle lies a hint of truth,
As we dance on dreams of tender youth.

Yet underneath, the jokes collide,
As humor masks the tears we hide.
From twinkling woes, we break the night,
With witty quips, we learn to fight.

So here's to glee and sorrow's touch,
Where laughter reigns, it means so much.
In every jest, we find the light,
For even tears can bloom so bright.

A Jewel's Silent Confession

In a box, she lies so bright,
Sparkling like stars at night.
Yet when worn, a funny sight,
Wobbles left and wobbles right.

On her neck, she feels so bold,
But her chain? It's far too cold.
Every move, a story told,
Of adventures wrapped in gold.

Fancy parties, she's the star,
But oh dear, that clasp's a scar!
Every laugh, a neck-expanding jar,
Just pray she doesn't drop the spar.

Gems may twinkle, though they dread,
Silly tales in laughter spread.
In shiny chaos, love is bred,
A jewel's heart, mischief led.

Radiance Woven in Shadows

In a dim-lit room she gleams,
Silvy light, or so it seems.
Hiding secrets, catching dreams,
Plotting schemes with silver beams.

Jokes exchanged, with laughter loud,
She's the star, draws in the crowd.
The shadows cloak her playful shroud,
Watch out! She's both fierce and proud!

Her brilliance shines, a flashy tease,
But little does she know, with ease,
Her spark pulls pranks, ain't that a breeze?
Stealing hearts like thieving bees.

As she glimmers, stories blend,
Each tale a twist, each laugh a bend.
In the night's glow, friendships mend,
A shimmering world without an end.

The Weight of Gilded Dreams

Heavier dreams, in gold they are,
But when she wears them, it's bizarre.
With every laugh, a chasing star,
She finds her balance, how absurd, ajar!

Dancing light, she wobbles top,
Her jewels jingle, never stop.
A clumsy twirl, oh, what a flop!
Yet through the air, her spirits hop.

In this comedy of sparkle's plight,
She jests, she spins, her heart takes flight.
While glitter plays in cheerful night,
She laughs away the weight, delight!

With each misstep, she learns to fly,
Through laughter's lens, the world's awry.
Gold may weigh, but spirits high,
In gilded dreams, we all comply.

Shards of Beauty and Burden

Shattered gems on polished floor,
Each glimmer holds a secret lore.
With every shard, a chance to score,
But warned, dear friend, it's hard to ignore.

She flaunts her glamour, a quirky dance,
But oh! A tumble, there's no chance.
With shattered grace, she takes a stance,
While laughter bursts like bubbles prance.

In glitzy gowns, she wears a grin,
Yet hides the truth of where she's been.
A funny tale of loss and win,
Reflecting life's sharpness from within.

But beauty's shards can weave a tale,
In every laugh, she'll never fail.
For with her heart, she'll always sail,
Turning burden into a joyous trail.

Desire's Glimmer

A twinkle caught in the eye's dance,
Hoping for riches with just a glance.
But a shiny gleam can lead astray,
Turning life's gold to a dusky gray.

Lust for jewels in every purse,
Yet a fortune lost is the cruelest curse.
With dreams of grandeur wrapped up tight,
One spark of envy can dim the light.

Laughter echoes in the halls of gold,
While stories of riches are humorously told.
For every diamond that one might claim,
There's a jest waiting to light the flame.

So dance, you fools, in glitter and glow,
For what we seek, we rarely know.
In desire's glimmer, there's fun to find,
And laughter bubble fills all our minds.

Lament in Luxury

A lady sighed with pearls in her hair,
Wishing for more, she couldn't bear.
Her neighbor flaunted a brand-new style,
While she wore last year's in jeweled guile.

The waiter dropped her diamond plate,
Saying, "Madam, this will be fate!"
With laughter mixed in her sobpin' wails,
She cursed the day she bought those trails.

Luxurious fabric and a velvet seat,
Yet the taste of dreams? Oh, bittersweet!
Each crystal purchased came with a price,
She joked to herself, "Would it suffice?"

So raise your glass with a clink and cheer,
For what's a laugh without some tear?
In luxury's grip, we find our way,
Lamenting the fashion of yesterday.

Veil of Radiance

Beneath a shimmer that dazzles bright,
Lies a tale wrapped in playful fright.
For all that glimmers can lead to fun,
But sometimes a glitch makes you come undone.

A veil of brilliance adorns her face,
With a twitch of charm, she wins the race.
Yet the fabric snags on a doorknob tight,
Leaving her stuck in quite a sight.

With laughter trailing as her veil floats free,
The whole room watches, eyes wide with glee.
For moments like these, we live and we learn,
That veils may hide, but they also turn.

So wear your radiance with a wink of jest,
Embrace the silly, and you'll find the best.
Underneath laughter, let joy be your guide,
For life's little snafus are where fun can hide.

Splintered Adornments

In a box of treasures, oh what a sight,
A brooch with style, it gleamed so bright.
Yet with a stumble and a twist around,
Splintered adornments fell to the ground.

With crystal shards and laughter so loud,
She blamed the cat, a mischievous crowd.
"Where's my tiara?" she teased with a yawn,
As jewels scattered like leaves on the lawn.

A party awaited with glitz and glam,
But now her dress looked like a sham.
She chuckled at glitter that wouldn't obey,
And danced with splinters in a wobbly ballet.

So if life hands you a box of mess,
Turn it to laughter, nothing less!
For splintered adornments, a story make,
And in the folly, a joy will awake.

Unraveled Dreams

In a box, she found her fate,
A piece so grand, yet oh so late.
She wore it once, what a delight,
Now it twinkles, far from sight.

With every twist and every turn,
She struts like royalty, watch her learn.
But wait! A snag, her dress does cling,
"Oh dear," she laughs, "what will this bring?"

At parties, she's the shining star,
With tales of woe from near and far.
Admiring glances at her 'prize',
But little do they see the lies.

The shine is bright, but just so thin,
Each laugh a dance, each grin a win.
With mock grandeur, she spins and sways,
In her mind, glamor's the only phase.

Sentinels of Splendor

A charming glint upon her neck,
While in her bag, a hidden wreck.
She struts out, her head held high,
But still she wonders, why oh why?

The jewels they sparkle, the tales they weave,
Yet fabric fades and dreams deceive.
Each laugh echoes like a chime,
But truth be told, it's just a crime.

"Dear friends, it's rare!" she plays the part,
But deep inside, a heavy heart.
For what's a gem without its glow,
When life's more fun with tales of woe?

The sentinels of splendor stare,
As she pretends to not a care.
With each misstep, she trips with glee,
"Let's write my story, best seller, me!"

Shattered Dreams

She clasped the sparkles, all aglow,
Beneath her dress, dreams laid low.
With each red carpet step, she grins,
But reality creeps, and laughter spins.

The mirror shows a glam facade,
Not a flaw, just a charade.
"Oh look, a star!" the whispers say,
Yet in her heart, chaos does play.

A slip, a trip, the crowd gasps loud,
With shattered dreams, she meets the crowd.
Yet laughter bursts as she takes a bow,
"Let's call this art! Inspiration now!"

Each broken piece, a reason to cheer,
For mishaps are jewels on a path unclear.
And so she finds a comedic light,
Through fractured dreams, she'll take flight.

Golden Echoes

Once she flaunted in golden threads,
While life tossed mischief, it surely spreads.
In a world where sparkle meets the flab,
Each stumble turns into a fab blab.

"How chic!" they say with eyes aglow,
Not knowing her blunders, stealing the show.
In laughter's light, her troubles fade,
As she rules the room, her own charade.

With tales of lost gems and luck so rare,
She spins her yarns without a care.
For every mishap holds a golden charm,
And humor's embrace keeps her warm.

So let the echoes of laughter ring,
Within their heart, she's still the queen.
With twinkling tales and sparkly jest,
She finds her joy, and life is blessed.

Resplendence in Ruin

In tattered dress, she claims the floor,
With fragments of dreams, she asks for more.
The hearts they flutter, the laughs they burst,
In resplendence found, amidst the worst.

"Oh darling, see my dazzling flair!"
She twirls around, a charming scare.
With every snag, a giggle erupts,
Imagined glories, her spirit erupts.

The mishaps dance in a merry spin,
Among the pixels of where she's been.
For in every folly lies the jest,
To live with laughter is truly blessed.

So raise a toast! To jewels unseen,
In ruin, she reigns like a quirky queen.
With ruin and mischief, the best of all,
Her heart still shines through every fall.

Threads of Elegance and Regret

She donned her gems with flair,
But tripped on a curious stair.
The pearls went flying wide,
As laughter swelled inside.

A shimmer in the night, oh dear,
One's treasure turned to sheer veneer.
Her friends all gasped and cheered,
For elegance, she clearly steered.

Whispers of Enchantment

A charming piece that shone so bright,
Made heads turn left and then to right.
But listen closely, oh my friend,
What glitters often meets its end.

With every twirl, the stories spun,
Of magic that was never fun.
And yet she smiled, despite the strife,
For laughter, sweetly wove her life.

Chain of Illusions

A loop of dreams around her neck,
A twist of fate, a comic wreck.
Each crystal held a tale untold,
Of whimsy and of fortune bold.

They danced around like playful sprites,
Misleading hearts on misty nights.
For every link, a chuckle brewed,
In chaos, joy was often viewed.

The Sparkling Veil of Longing

She wore a gown of glittered wishes,
While leaping over rainy dishes.
Each sparkle twinkled with delight,
Yet hid the woes, both day and night.

A veil that shimmered with a grin,
Despite the price of what's within.
In laughter's glow, she found her way,
Crafting joy from disarray.

Embrace of Elegance

A lady lost her precious bling,
She searched the house, the car, the ring.
Her husband chuckled, said with glee,
"It's only diamonds, don't fret, dear me!"

She wore a smile, a borrowed sheen,
While her friends laughed, 'Oh, what a scene!'
With every sparkle that she pretended,
A drama formed, humor unended.

In cafes, she bragged of things so rare,
Yet all along, it was just hot air.
Toasting glasses filled with air so light,
Such elegance shone, a comical sight!

But in a twist, the jig was up,
Her husband claimed a wild hiccup.
"More precious than jewels, this love we flaunt,
Now, can you lend me some of that carefree jaunt?"

Secrets Beneath the Surface

In a box, she tucked her dreams,
A secret stash of golden beams.
With every glance, she'd squeal with pride,
'Oh darling, see what's deep inside!'

Yet one fateful day, the box popped wide,
And out flew all the hopes she'd tried.
Her cat wore pearls, a crown of grace,
While her husband just shook his face!

"What's worth is false?" he teased and laughed,
As she grinned, a scheming craft.
Her aspirations turned into fluff,
A comedy gem, oh isn't it tough?

So now they giggle under the stars,
Trading dreams like candy bars.
Her hidden treasures, nothing but fun,
As they watched their laughter almost outrun.

Heirloom of Aspirations

An heirloom passed through desperate hands,
Tales of grandeur from distant lands.
"It's worth a fortune!" they'd claim with zest,
Yet in reality, it's just a jest!

In parties, she'd flaunt her artifact bright,
While folks would snicker, what a sight!
"Is it gold? Is it bronze?" they'd quiz with charm,
"O dear," she'd grin, "It's an heirloom of harm!"

A whisper here, a laugh up there,
She'd dance around, bare feet in the air.
With every glance, she'd wink and say,
"Who needs the truth? Let's play this way!"

And so, her aspirations shone through,
As became a legend, well overdue.
For in the tales, her heart would beat,
A joyous farce, oh what a treat!

Luminous Lies

Strung along with tales so bright,
She grinned and sparkled in the night.
"Are they real?" a whisper passed,
She laughed, "Oh dear, nothing's ever cast!"

In chandeliers of glimmering grace,
She'd waltz with laughter, light on her face.
The crowd fought hard to keep it cool,
While she juggled mischief like a fool!

A magic trick, a twist of fate,
She wore that story like a cape.
With every glance, she beckoned delight,
"Would you care to join this luminous flight?"

So here's to lies that sparkle and shine,
For in our hearts, they intertwine.
With goofy giggles, we play the part,
And toast to tales that light the heart!

Captivating Alchemy

A shiny trinket caught my eye,
Its shimmer made me want to cry.
Thought I'd find great wealth in time,
But it turned out just a silly crime.

I wore it out to impress the crowd,
Spinning tales, feeling proud.
But with each wink, the whispers grew,
"Is it real? Or just a tootle-dee-doo?"

I danced and pranced, a sight to see,
With laughter as my currency.
But a slight tug, and it went PLOP!
Into the soup! We all just stopped!

Now I savor laughs over fine cuisine,
That pendant was never truly supreme.
In my heart, I learned one song:
Funny tales are where we belong!

Ode to Opulence

An elegant piece glimmered bright,
I thought it'd make my day and night.
Strutting like a fancy crow,
Turns out I'm just a class-A show!

With jeweled dreams, I took the stage,
To act my part, and feel the rage.
But when I tripped, and down I fell,
It turned to giggles, oh what a swell!

My friends said, "Gems don't win the race,"
But laughter? That's a ballsy place.
A sparkly blunder, a moment bright,
Opulence couldn't match this flight!

So here's to bling and laughter's charm,
A simple mishap does no harm.
For in the end, it's not the gold,
But funny tales that we hold!

Visions in Velvet

Draped in grand fabric, oh so fine,
Wearing riches I thought divine.
But hidden beneath that lovely sheen,
Was a secret that made me keen.

I twirled and spun, what a delight,
But then tripped on a shoe too tight.
Velvet reached out like a great big hug,
Caught me off guard, I took a shrug!

"Did it cost a fortune?" they would say,
As I laughed my royal ballet.
The vision blurred, though not too grand,
For laughter is the wealth at hand!

So here's to velvet and its charm,
Life's silliness keeps us warm.
With each mishap, I take my stand,
Just a star in my own silly band!

Echoes of Echoes

In a hall of mirrors, shiny and wide,
Each reflection couldn't run and hide.
I donned my treasure, with sparkle anew,
But what I saw? A hilarious view!

Echoes of giggles danced all around,
My grand display turned into a clown.
With every pose, I struck a chance,
To trip, to slip, to do the dance!

"Did you see that?" a friend would shout,
Laughter erupted, no room for doubt.
I posed for glory, but in a blink,
In fun, I learned to let go and not think!

So here's my treasure, not gold or bling,
But the laughter and joy that they bring.
Echoes of echoes, I hear them cheer,
In silliness, I'll hold them dear!

www.ingramcontent.com/pod-product-compliance
Lightning Source LLC
Chambersburg PA
CBHW060144230426
43661CB00003B/558